YOU CHOOSE

Life in the INDUS CIVILIZATION

AN INTERACTIVE ANCIENT HISTORY ADVENTURE

BY ERIC BRAUN

Consultant:
Dr. Marta Ameri
Associate Professor, Department of Art
Colby College, Waterville, Maine

CAPSTONE PRESS
a capstone imprint

Published by Capstone Press, an imprint of Capstone
1710 Roe Crest Drive, North Mankato, Minnesota 56003
capstonepub.com

Copyright © 2026 by Capstone. All rights reserved. No part of this publication may be reproduced in whole or in part, or stored in a retrieval system, or transmitted in any form or by any means, electronic, mechanical, photocopying, recording, or otherwise, without written permission of the publisher.

Library of Congress Cataloging-in-Publication Data
is available on the Library of Congress website.

ISBN: 9798875216336 (hardcover)
ISBN: 9798875216305 (paperback)
ISBN: 9798875216312 (ebook PDF)

Summary: The Indus Civilization thrived in a river valley in South Asia for thousands of years. Its culture was known for its sophisticated and well-organized cities, as well as its reliance on agriculture and peaceful trade with its neighbors. But what was it like to live there during the height of this civilization? Explore life as a teen starting a new career. Try your hand as a traveling trader. Work as a builder in a growing city. YOU CHOOSE who to be, where to go, and what to do. Will you succeed? Will you fail? Will you even survive? It's up to you!

Editorial Credits
Editor: Chris Harbo; Designer: Bobbie Nuytten;
Media Researcher: Svetlana Zhurkin; Production Specialist: Katy LaVigne

Image Credits
Alamy: Jan Traylen, 84, Sabena Jane Blackbird, 48, wayfarer, 33; Getty Images: AFP/Ashraf Khan, 108, Dinodia Photo, 59, Dorling Kindersley, 68, imageBROKER/Michael Runkel, 91, Nadeem Khawar, 81, Sergey Strelkov, cover (middle); The Metropolitan Museum of Art: Dodge Fund, 1949, 109, Rogers Fund and Purchase, Joseph Pulitzer Bequest, by exchange, 1957, cover (bottom left), 37; Newscom: akg-images/Paul Almasy, 10, robertharding Productions, 16, Universal Images Group/QAI Publishing, 18; Shutterstock: Adnan_Gee, 98, AlexelA, 53, andreev-studio, 71, eyetravelphotos, 63, Ian Old (wooden doorway), cover, 1, itsswati, 40, MudaCom, 105, MysticaLink, 6–7 (rivers), PorcupenWorks, 6–7 (base map), Pravine, 24, Sergey-73, 4, Sheril Kannoth, 45, shozib ali brohi, 8, 12, 42, 46, 78, 102, Waqar rauf Zafer, 29

Any additional websites and resources referenced in this book are not maintained, authorized, or sponsored by Capstone. All product and company names are trademarks™ or registered® trademarks of their respective holders.

Printed and bound in China. 6276

TABLE OF CONTENTS

ABOUT YOUR ADVENTURE................ 5
GET TO KNOW THE INDUS
   CIVILIZATION....................... 6

Chapter 1
CLEAN AND ORDERLY................... 9

Chapter 2
FINDING YOUR PLACE IN
   MOHENJO-DARO..................... 13

Chapter 3
THE TRADER IN THE PORT............. 47

Chapter 4
HARAPPA LIFE....................... 79

Chapter 5
THE END OF THE INDUS CIVILIZATION . 103

   Timeline of the Indus Civilization....... 106
   More About the Indus Civilization 107
   The Indus Civilization Today 108
   Glossary 110
   Read More 111
   Internet Sites 111
   About the Author 112
   Books in This Series 112

ABOUT YOUR ADVENTURE

YOU are living in the Indus Civilization in South Asia thousands of years ago. As a member of this thriving society, you want to do your part to support your family and community. You could be a teenager who must choose a career path. Or you may be a traveling trader who visits far off lands. You could also be a builder who constructs homes and other important buildings in your growing city.

Whatever you decide, YOU CHOOSE the paths that will fulfill your destiny or seal your fate. How will you make your mark as a member of this remarkable civilization?

Turn the page to begin your adventure.

Get to Know the
INDUS CIVILIZATION

The Indus Civilization was located in parts of modern-day India, Pakistan, and Afghanistan. It was at its peak from 2600–1900 BCE.

INDUS RIVER
CHENAB RIVER
RAVI RIVER
SUTLEJ RIVER
GHAGGAR-HAKRA RIVER

○ Harappa

Mohenjo-daro ○

○ Lothal

Kathiawar Peninsula

Mohenjo-daro had a Great Bath, a public pool that may have been used for purification rituals or simply as a social place to bathe.

Indus children played with toys such as model carts and animals made of clay.

ARABIAN SEA

Modern archaeologists have found well over 1,000 ancient cities and settlements in the area of the Indus Civilization.

Carved soapstone seals could be pressed into wet clay as a sign of ownership or responsibility.

The people of the Indus were known for their bead-making skills.

Indus buildings were made from mud and baked bricks of uniform size and shape.

Historians don't know very much about the Indus religion or language. Some texts exist on stone seals, pottery, and other artifacts such as a large signboard found in the city of Dholavira. But archaeologists haven't been able to decipher them yet.

BAY OF BENGAL

Chapter 1
CLEAN AND ORDERLY

YOU wake up in your bedroom, where sunlight and a cool breeze stream in the open window. You glance out the window and up at the blue sky. Puffy clouds float by, casting their shadows on the clean, orderly street down below. You get up and rub the sleep from your eyes. It's time to get ready for work.

You are a citizen of a peaceful city along the Indus River in South Asia thousands of years ago. Yours is one of hundreds of cities and towns making up a large civilization that is dependent on several rivers and many tributaries in the region. Your people use them for drinking water, sewage, bathing, and farming. When the rivers flood, they irrigate the crops and leave nutrient-rich silt to grow enough food for everyone in the cities to eat.

Your city is well-organized. The streets are laid out on a grid, and your home looks similar to every other home in town. It has two floors, separate living spaces, and a well where you can get fresh water. It also has a toilet that connects to underground sewage lines.

There is no standing army in your city or in the entire Indus Civilization—you are a peaceful people. But you are not self-sufficient. You trade with other civilizations to get what you need.

Mohenjo-daro was the largest city of the Indus Civilization.

At the bottom of the stairs, you dip a pail into the well. You pull up some cool, fresh water and pour a cupful. You drink half of it down, pausing to think about the day ahead. You know there is much work to do to run a major city like yours, and you are excited to do your part to help. It feels good to know you are contributing to your community as well as helping to care for your family.

Of course, there are dangers—every job has dangers—but there are also rewards. As you drink down the rest of your water, a small smile crosses your face. You feel lucky to live in one of the greatest civilizations on earth.

You say goodbye to your family and head out onto the bustling street.

> To be a teenager choosing a career, turn to page 13.
> To be a traveling trader, turn to page 47.
> To help build a growing city, turn to page 79.

Chapter 2

FINDING YOUR PLACE IN MOHENJO-DARO

"It is a big day!" your father exclaims as the two of you walk down the sunny street. He puts his arm around your shoulder. "Your first day of work. I'm so proud of you. Have you decided what you would like to do?"

You and your father live with your mother and younger sister in Mohenjo-daro, one of the largest cities in the Indus Valley. This lively metropolis has two main areas. The Lower Town is where most people, like you, live. The citadel, built on top of a huge mound, is where many public buildings are.

Turn the page.

You are old enough now that you're expected to help support the family. You have been excited for this day. It is fine being young, hanging out with friends, and going to school. But you are eager to start your career. The only question is, what job will you do?

Your parents earn their living in a metalworking shop. It would be easy to follow in their footsteps. You love the artistic statues and useful tools they've made your whole life. You can feel the work and expertise that went into the items they make just by holding them.

On the other hand, you have always admired your friend Harsha's family. They are hunters. Harsha himself recently joined the hunters and has bragged about spearing a gazelle. This work sounds exciting in a way that working inside on crafts can't match.

To make crafts, go to page 15.
To be a hunter, turn to page 17.

"I want to continue the tradition of our family," you tell your father proudly. "I want to craft things that others can use and enjoy."

Your father smiles broadly. "Wonderful," he says. "Follow me."

He pushes open the door to the workshop he shares with other craftspeople. The familiar smell of molten metal rushes out at you as you step into the busy room. You've been here many times to visit, but now it feels different. Now you are a part of it.

Your father makes a big deal of introducing you to the other workers. He tells them you will be learning how to do the work they do and eventually become an accomplished craftsperson. The people in the room smile back.

"Welcome!" says a man with dark skin and a heavy, black beard. You've met him before. His name is Sushruta.

Turn the page.

A bronze female statue found at a Mohenjo-daro excavation site

Sushruta is famous all over the city for his artistic creations. A copper statue of a dancing girl he made is displayed in your own home.

"We are pleased to have you with us," Sushruta says. "Would you like to join me for your first project?"

It would be an honor to work with such a talented and famous sculptor. Of course, your own father is quite well-regarded himself. He makes some of the sturdiest, most useful tools in the city.

To make art with Sushruta, turn to page 20.
To craft a tool with your father, turn to page 21.

"You know I love the work you do," you tell your father. "I may want to be an artisan like you someday. But hunting with Harsha sounds so exciting."

Your father keeps walking, and you can't read his expression. Have you disappointed him? After a moment, he speaks up.

"I think that is a good idea. If you are a strong hunter, you will bring honor to our family. And you can always change your mind later."

You thank your father for understanding and say goodbye as he steps into his metalworking shop. Then you run two blocks north and six blocks east to Harsha's house. You arrive out of breath just as he is stepping outside with a long spear in hand.

"Hello!" he says. "Are you here to join the hunt?"

Turn the page.

"I am, Harsha. Let's go!"

You and your friend walk one block north and then head west on a wide, clean main road. Soon, you reach the mound and climb the stairs to the upper part of town. Then you continue to another set of stairs and climb them. At the top of the stairs, a large rectangular pool is surrounded by brick columns.

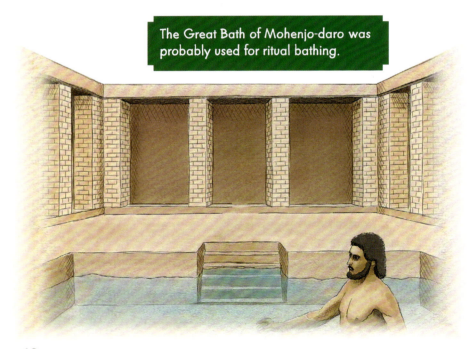

The Great Bath of Mohenjo-daro was probably used for ritual bathing.

You and Harsha remove your clothes. Then you walk down brick steps and into the water for a solemn moment of meditation. This is a religious "cleansing ritual" that all the hunters perform before starting a hunt.

When you are finished, you meet the other hunters outside the Great Bath. You and your friend are the youngest there.

A tall, strong-looking man hands you a long spear like Harsha's. "We have two expeditions today," the man says. Then he goes on to explain that one group will hunt gazelles. They are difficult and dangerous to kill because of their speed and their horns. The other group will be hunting rabbits, which are abundant outside the city walls. They are quick and small, making them difficult targets.

To hunt gazelles, turn to page 23.
To hunt rabbits, turn to page 26.

You think of Sushruta's statuette on display in your home and decide to try your hand at making beautiful art.

"Sushruta," you say, "I would be honored to learn from you."

Sushruta smiles and leads you toward his work area. Tools—such as large and small copper knives, spoons, hooks, different sized weights, and gloves—hang from the wall. He explains that beautiful beads your area is known for are cut and drilled using specialized tools, whereas bronze items are cast from the melted metal. In fact, the molten metal reaches incredible temperatures, and you must be careful not to burn yourself.

"I love working with both materials," Sushruta says. "And I will teach you both methods. Where shall we begin?"

To make beads, turn to page 28.
To cast something from bronze, turn to page 31.

"Thanks for the offer," you say to Sushruta. "But I'd like to make tools with my father."

"As you wish," Sushruta replies.

As he walks away, you spot an assortment of fishhooks hanging on a wall.

"I'd like to make those," you say.

"A fine choice," your father replies.

Moments later, you and your father settle in at the fishhook station. He shows you how to chop a sliver of copper from a larger piece using a hammer and chisel. You slim it down further with the chisel while your father stokes a large fire.

Next, you use a pair of tongs to hold the copper in the fire until it softens. When it's ready, you take it to an anvil and shape it into a hook. Then you fashion a hole on the opposite end to run a line through. When the hook cools, you use a whetstone to sharpen the tip.

Turn the page.

You look at some of the hooks on the wall. It's obvious yours isn't very good. This is to be expected, since it's your first try.

You repeat the process on a second hook, and it looks much the same. You make a third. You hold it up to the light. Is it better? It's not as straight as you would like, and you're not sure if the loop will hold up to a strong fish on the line.

Soon, your father comes to check in. He furrows his brow as he examines your work.

"Do another," he says.

Perhaps fishhooks are too difficult for a first project. It might make sense to work on something easier in order to sharpen your skills.

> To try the hooks again, turn to page 34.
> To try something else, turn to page 36.

You decide to hunt gazelles. You've played hunting games with your childhood friends in the past. You've always enjoyed the idea of hunting a fast, challenging target. Soon, you and Harsha join the hunting party heading to the north end of the city.

Once you reach a river outside of town, you and Harsha practice throwing your spears at a tree. Your friend has gotten much better since your younger days playing games. His throws are not only harder and faster than yours, but much more accurate. You feel a tinge of jealousy, but you remind yourself that you are here to learn and improve. If anything, Harsha's ability is a hint of what you will be able to do someday.

A short time later, you follow the hunting group upriver. The men in front walk quietly and swiftly, and you try to do the same.

Turn the page.

Soon, you reach a curve in the river, where a broad meadow opens up ahead of you. The water at this bend tumbles over rocks and crashes loudly. Its noise masks your group's approach. Above the rapids is a calm pool where gazelles are known to drink and rest.

As you walk, the leader of your group flashes the signal to stop. Up ahead, four gazelles stand on the other side of the river. The leader points to you. He wants you to take the first shot.

Indian gazelles

Since the animals are across the river, they are near the limit of your throwing range. To get any closer, you'd have to cross the river, which means they might hear you and flee. But if you throw from here, you're not confident that you can hit them.

To try to get closer, turn to page 38.
To throw from here, turn to page 40.

You think hunting rabbits might be fun. They may be quick, but they will let you get closer than gazelles will. And rabbits can't gore you with horns like a gazelle can.

A short time later, you go through a gate and step outside the city walls. Your hunting group walks toward a grove of trees, and soon you see dozens of rabbits. They sit on their haunches munching grass.

You zero in on the one closest to you. Its jaws stop moving as you draw near. It has its eye on you. You reach back with your spear. The rabbit doesn't move. Then you unleash a mighty throw!

Your violent motion scares the rabbit. As it dashes away, your spear strikes the ground where it was standing. It was an accurate throw, but too late.

The remaining rabbits scatter into the woods as you run toward your spear. As you pull it from the ground, you see several rabbits have been hit by other hunters.

Wasting no time, you run in the direction the rabbits fled. You spot them munching on grass again, so you throw your spear. Once again, you miss while several of your peers hit their targets.

This happens all day long. While other hunters are collecting meat, you are just chasing your spear around. As your elbow throbs from all the throws, you wonder if you'd have been better off as an artisan.

THE END

To follow another path, turn to page 11.
To learn more about the Indus Civilization,
turn to page 103.

Making beads seems safer than working with molten metals, and you like the idea of seeing your progress with each bead. Sushruta helps you choose a piece of quartz and hands you a thin bronze saw. Then he shows you a safe technique for making the cuts.

The stone is hard, and you have to be careful you don't slip and slice your hand as you work. But little by little, the bead takes shape. It is a beautiful red color. Soon, Sushruta shows you how to drill a hole in the bead using a tiny copper drill. Finally, you carefully shape the bead by sanding it.

The first day you only make the one bead, but on day two you are working with more confidence. You make three more beads, and Sushruta smiles and nods as he walks past. They look good. After a couple weeks, you string together a necklace of many beads.

Beaded necklaces on display at a Mohenjo-daro museum

Next time your family goes to the market, you take your necklace. You compare your necklace to those of others, and you notice that many other artisans have crafted finer, tinier beads, and many have fine lines etched into them. Only the very best craftspeople can make beads so small, intricately designed, and beautifully shaped.

Turn the page.

At first, people don't look at your beads. But finally, an older woman stops and picks up your necklace. She holds it up and pulls the beads through her fingers. Then she reaches into a bag and pulls out a small clay bowl.

"I'll give you this for the beads," she says in a kind voice.

You were hoping for more, but realize this is probably the best offer you'll get. You accept her bowl and give it to your family for serving grains. Your mother thanks you, and the smile on her face makes it all worthwhile.

When you return to the workshop, you get to work carving your next string of beads. You're determined to make them smaller and more lovely, and you can't wait until Sushruta teaches you how to etch designs into them.

THE END

To follow another path, turn to page 11.
To learn more about the Indus Civilization, turn to page 103.

Casting bronze is dangerous work, but you are excited to try it. You've always admired people who work with molten metal.

You start with an existing model of a running buffalo. You coat the model with clay to form a box around it. Then you slide the clay box into an oven called a kiln to bake.

Once the clay box is baked, you slide it out and let it cool. Then you cut the box in half, remove the model, and place the two clay halves together again. The box is now a mold.

Next, you drill a hole in the top of the mold and pour melted wax inside it. You turn the mold to make sure the wax coats every corner, then you set it aside until the wax hardens.

Later that day, you pull the two halves of the mold apart to reveal a wax buffalo. You use a sharp tool to engrave flowing hair and other fine details into the wax. Then you coat the wax model with clay to create the final mold.

Turn the page.

You drill a hole in the cube-shaped mold and then bake it until the wax melts and drains out the hole. Meanwhile, in a separate fire, you heat copper and other metals, such as tin and arsenic, until they boil and become bronze.

You place the empty mold on the floor. Then you carefully pour the molten bronze into the mold's hole.

"Hold it strong and steady," Sushruta says.

You sweat as the superhot metal fills the mold to the top. But you manage to complete the task without getting a nasty burn. Now, you wait.

The next morning you wake up early and arrive at the workshop bursting with excitement. You use a hammer and chisel to carefully break the mold apart. As the chunks fall away, a bronze statuette is revealed. The running buffalo looks realistic and beautiful.

A bronze bull from the Indus Civilization

"Can I keep it?" you ask your father. You are very proud of your piece of art.

"It is beautiful," your father says. "But we must take it to the market tomorrow. We will be able to trade it for cotton to make blankets. We might even get more raw metals to make more artwork."

You know he is right. As much as you'd like to keep your first piece of art, trading it will be a big help to your family.

THE END

To follow another path, turn to page 11.
To learn more about the Indus Civilization,
turn to page 103.

"I will keep trying," you tell your father. You know the only way to get better is to practice.

Again, you cut a sliver of copper and heat it over the fire. You pull it out and bend it into a hook. Suddenly, it snaps in two. Your father is watching, so you hide your frustration and try again.

The next hook is better. You sharpen it, and you like how it looks. You do another one, and it looks even better. By the end of the day, you have three hooks that you believe can work.

After dinner that evening, you take one of your hooks to the river to test it out. You are surprised when you snag something heavy in the water. After a fight of several minutes, you pull in a large catfish.

"Yahoo!" you yell out. You slip the fish into a woven basket and bring it home. "Look what I caught with my own hook!" you exclaim.

"Wonderful," says your mother. "I will smoke it tonight, and tomorrow you can eat it for breakfast."

"You should keep making fishhooks," your father says. "You have a knack for it."

THE END
To follow another path, turn to page 11.
To learn more about the Indus Civilization, turn to page 103.

You decide to try making something else. After pondering for a minute, you remember that your friend Harsha broke one of his family's baking pots last week. His family needs a new one. In fact—you realize—many families probably need new pots!

Using clay, you shape a large pot and smooth its sides with your wet hands. You shape a lip at the top, and then you slide it into an oven called a kiln to bake until it hardens.

When you remove it later, you smile. The pot is handsome and useful. Using a small brush, you paint a creature on the side of the pot. It looks like a combination of a bull and a unicorn—a creature that graces many seals and pieces of pottery in your city. You also add some personal flourishes along the rim such as a flowery vine.

A clay pot with painted decoration from the Indus Civilization

When the pot is done, you set it on a low shelf and admire it. Right away, you start on another one. You figure you can make a dozen pots or more in a few days. You'll give one to Harsha as a gift and trade the others for meat or spices for your family.

THE END

To follow another path, turn to page 11.
To learn more about the Indus Civilization, turn to page 103.

You think you'll have a better shot if you sneak up on the gazelles. You stay out of sight as you crouch below the reeds and cattails along the riverbank. Then you peer through the foliage.

Suddenly, one of the gazelles lifts its head. Does it smell you? You freeze, and the gazelle seems to relax.

You wait a moment before taking another couple steps. Unfortunately, you step into a pool of water covered by weeds. The splash startles the gazelles, and they gallop away.

You dash into the river and launch your spear, but it's not even close. The gazelles run out of range.

You trudge across the river to pick up your spear. You're grumpy and wet. Not only that, a couple of men in your hunting party are looking at you with disgust. Because of your clumsiness, you've let them down.

Maybe you should return to the city, so you don't ruin the entire hunt. You could try another trade. On the other hand, it would be humiliating to quit—and your friend Harsha might even laugh at you.

> To try a different trade, turn to page 42.
> To keep hunting, turn to page 44.

You can't risk getting closer—the gazelles will certainly see or hear you. Then they will get away. You will have to try throwing your spear from here. You've always had a strong arm, and you believe you can do it.

You reach back and throw your spear at the nearest gazelle. You've hit it!

Then you realize your spear struck the hind leg instead of the chest. The gazelle is injured, but strong enough to run.

Ancient hunting arrows at a museum in Lothal in present-day India

As the herd scatters, you chase after your limping target. Even though it is hurt, it is still faster than you. Soon, it's out of sight.

You and Harsha track the gazelle by following blood stains and hoof prints on the ground. It takes hours, but finally, just after dark, you catch up to it. The animal is lying in some short grass, panting and bleeding. You pull your knife from your belt and finish the job.

Harsha helps you carry the animal back to the city. It is late at night by the time you get there, and nobody is awake to celebrate your moment of glory.

THE END

To follow another path, turn to page 11.
To learn more about the Indus Civilization,
turn to page 103.

Even though Harsha might laugh at you for quitting, you know you need to try something else. You're just not cut out to be a hunter, and if you continue to try you will make it difficult for your hunting party.

On the way home, you see a farmer on the side of the road with a broken wagon wheel. You quickly figure out the problem and use some of the farmer's spare wood and tools to repair the wheel. Soon, he is happily leading his zebu and wagon away.

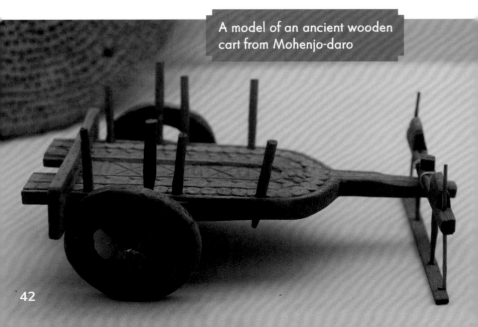

A model of an ancient wooden cart from Mohenjo-daro

That night, you tell your father that you would like to try something besides hunting. He asks if you would like to be an artisan like him, but you have another idea. You think you would be good at working on wagons and farm equipment. You tell him about the farmer you helped today, and he nods.

"Yes," he says. "You have always been mechanically-minded. I know a man who will take you in to work with him. We will go there tomorrow."

You lay in bed that night and think about your day. In spite of the embarrassing hunting mishaps, it was a good one. You are on your way to becoming an adult who will contribute to the community.

THE END
To follow another path, turn to page 11.
To learn more about the Indus Civilization,
turn to page 103.

You don't want to face your family or your friend as a quitter, so you dash off after the gazelles. You know you shouldn't leave your hunting party, but you're determined to get one. You push through some high grass that is bent—evidence that the gazelles passed this way. When you reach a clearing, you see them grazing on the far side. With a mighty heave, you throw your spear—and miss again!

You grumble to yourself in frustration as you are retrieving your spear. Suddenly, you feel a sharp pain in your leg. Looking down, you see a long, spectacled cobra slithering away from you. It must have bit you!

You can't believe it. You were so distracted by your disappointment in yourself that you weren't being careful about your surroundings. Your heart sinks. You are in great danger now. You call for help, but the other hunters are far away. You call again.

spectacled cobra

The sky quickly turns dark—did night come on fast, or is this the effect of the cobra's venom? You can't be sure. But you feel very tired, and you close your eyes.

Maybe you can just rest here a moment while you wait for help.

THE END

To follow another path, turn to page 11.
To learn more about the Indus Civilization, turn to page 103.

Chapter 3
THE TRADER IN THE PORT

As you step outside your home, the smell of saltwater and fish wafts around you. You love that smell—you grew up here in this port city of Lothal, on the Arabian Sea. And though you travel a great deal for your job as a trader, you're always happy to return home.

As you hitch your zebus to your cart, you look at the covered drainage system along the sides of the street. It rained overnight, and they have done their job perfectly by channeling water off the streets and toward the ocean. The hard mud bricks beneath your feet remain stiff in spite of getting wet overnight.

Turn the page.

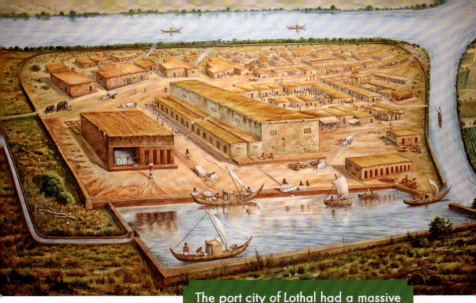

The port city of Lothal had a massive dockyard, one of the greatest works of ancient maritime architecture.

Today you are heading out of town on a long trading journey. You bid goodbye to your spouse and your children as you climb into the cart.

"Yah!" you yell. The zebus strain briefly against their harness before pulling the cart out into the busy street.

To travel by sea to Mesopotamia, go to page 49.
To travel by land to Iran, turn to page 52.

Before starting your long journey to Mesopotamia by sea, you have an important errand to run. You steer your cart to the shop of a local craftsman down near the docks. As you come to a stop, seagulls cry above and waves slosh against the nearby rocks.

On your last voyage overseas, your men had to row the entire way. This time, you've hired a local craftsman named Gupta to sew a sail for you. Although sails are a relatively new invention, you've learned how to use one while traveling on other boats. And you've heard that Gupta is the best sailmaker in the business. The new sail will cost you a lot, but it will help your boat move faster.

As you climb out of the cart, Gupta comes out of his workshop with large shears in his hands.

"Come inside!" he calls excitedly. "Come see!"

Turn the page.

You follow Gupta through the shop and into a courtyard in back. Once there, he unfolds a large sail. It is beautiful and looks strong. You pay him, and he helps you carry the sail to your cart. Then you ride to the dock where your large, flat-bottomed boat awaits. With the help of your crew, you rig up the sail.

As you prepare to set out, you check your cargo. Your boat is carrying a heavy load of copper and pottery pieces. As your crew rows your boat out of the harbor, you smile. You'll make a fortune trading this valuable cargo. You hug the shore as you travel, eventually raising the sail to let the wind do the work.

The first several days of your trip are beautiful and sunny. But late in the second week of travel, you get nervous. Dark clouds are up ahead, and the wind is picking up. Sure enough, a storm is soon on top of you.

The rain comes down in heavy sheets, and the sail snaps loudly in the whipping wind. The boat rocks and tosses on the high waves. Your men look to you to make a decision.

You don't want to lose a travel day, but it would be safer to head for shore and wait out the storm until morning. On the other hand, you know there is a protected gulf not too far ahead. Once you reach it, you'll be safe from the storm. Maybe you should chance it.

To head for shore, turn to page 55.
To push for the gulf, turn to page 57.

You guide your zebus to the warehouse next to your home. Your plan is to travel to Iran to trade cotton. It's a resource the Indus Valley is rich in—and your warehouse is stocked with it. Inside you have large stores of raw cotton as well as dyed fabric and articles of clothing.

Soon, three workers join you with another wagon. The four of you load the two wagons with the goods. You also pack food, blankets, and jugs of water for your journey.

About an hour later, you pass through the city gates and join a caravan of about a dozen other merchants. Then you all head north on a well-traveled road along the shore. Your cart rocks and squeaks as the zebus pull it along. Your second cart follows behind you.

That night, you camp just off the road. Early the next morning you wake up, eat some dried fish and bread, and get going right away.

A modern statue of a pair of zebus pulling a loaded cart in Mohenjo-daro

The next several days are as uneventful as the first. But as you're about to make camp near a well-traveled intersection that evening, you hear people traveling from another direction. You know that some parts of towns in the area have been experiencing troubles with attackers. Some trade routes have been disrupted.

Turn the page.

The caravan stops. A man from the lead cart walks back to talk to the driver of every cart. When he gets to you, he says, "Many of the men are concerned. They fear an attack by bandits."

As an older veteran of the route, you are well respected among the men. They are looking to you to make a decision.

You could keep going another couple miles to avoid whoever is coming toward the intersection. If it's bandits, you will be pretty much defenseless. While you have some hunting spears, you are not a warlike people. You don't have weapons or fighting skills. Then again, the other people approaching may just be traders like you. If you stay put, you could exchange news and try to trade with them.

If you move on a little farther to hide, turn to page 59.

If you stay put, turn to page 61.

"Let's get off this water," says Farouk, your first mate. "The men are worried."

You agree. You bank toward shore and begin rowing hard. The closer you get, the worse the storm grows. Water and wind lash the boat. As lightning flashes and thunder roars, you're glad that you decided to play it safe.

As soon as you hit land, everyone jumps out to pull the boat ashore. Near the edge of the beach, you set up camp under a line of trees. Everyone is soaked and shivering, and nobody sleeps much at all.

The next morning, you are thrilled to wake up to the sun blaring down on you. As your men eat dried fish, you check your cargo. Remarkably, it all looks good.

While breaking camp and loading your boat, you see another boat heading your way. You wait for them to make landfall in case they have anything to trade.

Turn the page.

"Hello!" says the captain as he wades toward you through the water. He tells you of their terrible night at sea in the storm. His men look exhausted and sick.

"We plan to take a couple days to rest here before heading back out," the captain explains. He also says they are planning to trade with a community farther up the coast. Then he eyes your copper statuettes. "I could do well trading some of those," he says.

"What do you have to offer?" you ask.

He produces a bag full of blue stones, both large and small. They are called lapis lazuli. They are beautiful and unlike anything you've ever seen before.

To trade some of your copper statuettes for lapis lazuli, turn to page 63.

To pass on trading, turn to page 65.

"Let's head for shore," says Farouk, your first mate. "We will only lose one day."

But you shake your head. "We continue," you say. "We can make the gulf."

You adjust the sail to catch the thrashing wind, and the men row as hard as they can. A small ray of sunshine peeks through a crack in the clouds, and you feel some hope. But then the crack closes and it's darker than before.

Suddenly, a bolt of lightning strikes the mast. The sail catches fire! You and your men quickly untie it and throw it off the boat. Your heart sinks as it flutters away and settles on the swells.

"We're taking on a lot of water!" Farouk yells over the noise of the battering rain and wind.

Turn the page.

He's right. You're standing in more than a foot of water, and it's rising fast. You start to worry you might sink. You could throw some of the precious pottery and copper goods overboard to make the boat lighter. You would go faster and the boat would ride higher on the water. But it would be very costly. Your trip to Mesopotamia might turn out to be a bust.

To throw some goods overboard, turn to page 67.

To press on with all your cargo, turn to page 70.

"It's better to be safe," you say. "Let's move on—fast."

The man agrees and spreads the word to other caravan drivers. Soon, you pass through the intersection and into a canyon beyond. You travel a couple miles and set up camp around a bend in the canyon.

All night long, a lookout keeps watch while the rest of you sleep. But no other travelers pass by. In the morning, you set off again.

Hilly landscape of the Kathiawar Peninsula in present-day India

Turn the page.

By late morning, you spot a small gathering of carts and tents up ahead. Since this group is much smaller than yours, you approach them without worry. That's when you realize this is an outpost market.

This group of merchants has lots of goods that you'd like to trade for, such as grains and colorful fruits. And trading with them would allow you to turn home now instead of completing the long journey to Iran. But you also know the prices here will be higher. That's the cost of convenience.

To trade here at the outpost, turn to page 71.
To keep going, turn to page 73.

"Let's stay put," you say.

The man agrees, and your caravan moves off the road to set up camp. As you start cooking, you hear rolling wheels getting closer. Soon, you hear voices in a language you don't recognize. Well after dark, a caravan of travelers arrives from the north. Your group keeps a watchful eye as they set up camp a hundred yards away. You can tell they are checking you out as well.

A short time later, five men from the other party walk over to your camp. They are armed with swords, shields, pikes, and knives. But they hold their hands out to show they mean you no harm.

You welcome the men into camp and offer them food and drink. After they eat, they get down to business. Using hand gestures, they make it clear they want to trade weapons for cotton.

Turn the page.

"This is a terrible offer," one of your men says. "They think we are stupid."

It's true that the amount of goods they're offering is way less valuable than what they are asking for. Besides, as a peaceful people, you have little use for their weapons. It's a bad trade all around.

"What if they don't like being rejected?" says another man. "They could slaughter us and take everything."

Perhaps you should accept their offer. It might be safer to keep them happy and prevent them from attacking you.

> To trade for weapons, turn to page 74.
> To decline the trade, turn to page 76.

Lapis lazuli has been used for making jewelry since ancient times.

The lapis lazuli is so beautiful that you think it will trade well in the Mesopotamian markets. You offer a large amount of copper goods in exchange for their entire trove of the blue stone. To your delight, they agree.

The rest of your journey to Mesopotamia is quick and easy. When you arrive a couple weeks later, you set up a stall at a bazaar.

Turn the page.

Your pottery goes quickly. You trade it for a normal amount of gold and silver. The people back home will use both of these metals for jewelry, statuettes, and tools.

But when you bring out the lapis lazuli, you get more attention than ever before. You are swarmed by locals who are stunned by the beautiful blue stone. You trade it for even better returns than you got for the copper. You stock up on cooking oils, wool, clothing, spices, and jewelry.

You made a good move trading for the lapis lazuli. You and your men will be heading home much wealthier than you were when you left.

THE END

To follow another path, turn to page 11.
To learn more about the Indus Civilization, turn to page 103.

You don't know if the blue stone is really worth anything. You've traded decorative stone before, but got less for it than more reliable goods such as copper. So, you decide to keep your copper, which you know the Mesopotamians will want.

You continue your journey until you land in a bustling city. You meet a merchant at a bazaar and agree to trade your copper for several beautiful clay jugs filled with olive oil from Greece. You also get some valuable grains and spices.

As you lug your items back to your boat, you pass a merchant selling lapis lazuli. You stop to observe their transactions, and you notice that they are making much better deals than you did with your copper. It turns out that the Mesopotamians value the blue stone quite highly—more highly than copper or pottery.

Turn the page.

Your heart sinks. You could have done a lot better had you come here with the beautiful stone.

As you load your boat, Farouk grabs you by the shoulder. "You fool," he hisses. "We could have gotten rich!"

He's right, of course. But now that you know the truth, you will do better next time.

THE END

To follow another path, turn to page 11.
To learn more about the Indus Civilization, turn to page 103.

Some of the men are terrified. You realize if you don't do something now, you could face a mutiny. Reluctantly, you give the order.

"One half of the cargo goes over!" you yell over the sounds of the storm.

The men eagerly obey. Working together, they heave half of the pots, jugs, bowls, and other clay items into the sea, as well as half of the copper tools and decorative figurines. To your relief, it works. With the reduced weight, the boat rises slightly. Most of the waves slap against the side instead of sloshing in.

The storm continues to pound your boat. You huddle against the onslaught and wait it out, tossing and flopping on the huge waves. But your heart is heavy because you have very little left to trade with. In fact, the trip will be practically a waste.

Then you hear a funny sound. *Flap!* Then another! *Flap!* And more! *Flap! Flap! Slap!*

Turn the page.

A trading ship from the Indus Civilization

The wild storm has caused several large fish to leap out of the water. Some even leap right into the boat! Already, half a dozen fish flop around on your deck.

Instantly, you realize you could salvage your trip if you can net enough fish to trade. Even though the conditions are still dangerous, you think the storm will break soon.

"Get the nets!" you command.

The men do so, and they quickly start pulling in nets full of fish. But as the boat tosses in the waves, Farouk falls overboard.

You lean out over the edge of the boat, but you can't see him in the churning water and pouring rain. Before long, you can't hear him scream, either.

Finally, you find land and spend a day drying the fish in the sun. Everyone feels gloomy because of Farouk, but eventually you continue your journey to Mesopotamia.

When you arrive, you trade the fish for some barley and other grains. You also trade for cooking oils and fruits. While you would have gotten a lot more for your copper and pottery, this is better than nothing.

As you head home, you dread telling Farouk's family he died in the storm. Perhaps he'd have lived if you hadn't been so focused on wealth.

THE END

To follow another path, turn to page 11.
To learn more about the Indus Civilization, turn to page 103.

"We can make it!" you yell.

You and the men strain at the oars. You fight the wind, the waves, and all the extra weight from the water filling the boat. Soon, water flows over the gunwales freely. The bow briefly dips underwater and rises again. When it dips once more, you are swept off your feet. The next thing you know, you are swimming in the sea.

Men yell and cry all around you, but it's hard to see where they are. You swim in a direction you think has land, but it's impossible to be sure. You swim as hard as you can, but it's no use. Your muscles begin to cramp. You get a mouthful of water. Then another. It's hard to stay up, and you realize the end is near.

THE END

To follow another path, turn to page 11.
To learn more about the Indus Civilization,
turn to page 103.

The prices at this outpost might be higher, but you like the idea of trading now and heading home sooner. And a shorter journey means less travel costs. So, you decide to look at what they have to offer.

These traders offer tin, which can be used to make bronze back home. After you trade some of your fine cotton clothes for the tin, you notice they have fine cotton clothes as well. Their designs are so beautiful and different, you trade the rest of your cotton clothes for theirs. You're certain the people back home will love the fresh looks.

tin ore

Turn the page.

After you complete the trades, you stamp your personal soapstone marker into a clay tablet as a receipt. Your marker shows a bull and some writing to identify your family.

Now it's time for you and the rest of the caravan to head home. As you guide your cart along the winding path, you let your mind wander. Could you have gotten a lot more for your goods if you had traveled farther? Perhaps. But you can always work extra hard in the future to make up for the loss.

THE END

To follow another path, turn to page 11.
To learn more about the Indus Civilization,
turn to page 103.

You didn't come this far only to pay high prices and go home with less. You'd rather press on to Iran. The outpost traders look at you with curiosity as your caravan passes by.

Two days later, you arrive at a large city. You set up in the market center, where you find great demand for your cotton. You trade for grains, colorful fruits, and precious metals. Because your cotton clothing is so popular, you are able to trade it for more than you would have gotten at the outpost.

After two days of heavy trading, you feel very happy. You made the right decision to press on, and now you'll bring home lots of useful goods for your family to use and trade.

To celebrate, you throw a big feast for your crew. The next day, you head for home.

THE END

To follow another path, turn to page 11.
To learn more about the Indus Civilization, turn to page 103.

You agree that it could be risky to reject these armed traders outright. So, you try to bargain with them.

You start by offering bolts of dyed cloth for swords you will never use. Their leader, a tall man wearing a sword and two knives on his belt, shakes his head. He points to a pile of sewed clothing and to the bolts of dyed cloth. Then he says something in his language.

You can't understand him, but you realize he is making a counteroffer. He wants the dyed cloth and several items of sewed clothing. In exchange, he offers several swords in leather scabbards and a handful of spears.

It's a terrible deal, but you're worried about what will happen if you refuse. Will he get angry and simply take what he wants?

Reluctantly, you accept his offer. Perhaps you can use the spears for hunting. Maybe you can resell the swords elsewhere.

Even if you can, though, you are coming out on the short end of the deal. What's worse, these traders will likely expect a similar deal the next time they see you on this road.

THE END

To follow another path, turn to page 11.
To learn more about the Indus Civilization,
turn to page 103.

You agree that it might be dangerous to refuse them. But if you make a bad trade with them now, it could destroy your reputation. If word spreads that you are afraid and will make bad trades, you'll face this situation more often in the future. So, you decide to stand firm.

"No," you say, shaking your head. It is a word that's easy to understand, even if you don't speak the same language. The leader of the group stands up and yells something at you. He is a burly man with sharp weapons hanging from his belt. Spittle flies from his mouth as he yells.

You cross your arms and shake your head again. "No."

One of the group's other men says something to the leader. Then the two of them begin to argue. Soon, all five of the men are bickering. But not long after that they return to their own camp.

The next morning, the other group is already gone by the time you pass through the intersection. When you arrive at a city in Iran a few weeks later, you see them in the market trading their weapons. You exchange nods of recognition before setting up your own stall.

Your cotton products are very popular here. You do well by trading for oxen, which will be a huge help for the farmers at home. And you're glad you stuck up for yourself. Now you can return home with pride.

THE END

To follow another path, turn to page 11.
To learn more about the Indus Civilization,
turn to page 103.

Chapter 4
HARAPPA LIFE

When you were a child, your family lived in a small village far upstream on the Ravi River, which flows into the Indus closer to the sea. Life there was simple but harder. The village's small population meant people had to grow and hunt food. They had to defend their families from attackers mostly on their own. Your family even had to build its own home and take care of one another when someone got sick or hurt.

Over the years, many families—including your own—left the village and moved to Harappa. This large city, which sits on the Ravi in the central part of the civilization, is home to thousands of people. And everyone here contributes to the greater good.

Turn the page.

In Harappa, a person can become an expert at one job instead of having to do everything. If someone gets sick, there is someone who knows how to help them. The city and surrounding area have experts in health care, building, farming, and more.

At first you were sad to move here because you had to leave your one good friend behind. But in time you made many new friends in Harappa. You also went to school to prepare for your role in the workforce.

In a city that continues to grow, there are many jobs you could do. But you want to do something that will help the city's new arrivals find a better life. That's why you've narrowed your job options down to being a builder or a farmer. You can either make new buildings or produce food to help feed everyone.

To be a builder, go to page 81.
To be a farmer, turn to page 83.

You love the idea of being a builder who adds new structures to the growing city. You join a crew that works together to create buildings where none existed before.

Your first project is to build a government building downtown. It has many different rooms and complicated plumbing to serve them. Although the work is hard, you quickly become close with your crew and make many friends. At night, you are exhausted and sleep well.

Harappa was the first city of the Indus Civilization excavated by archaeologists.

Turn the page.

When the government building is completed, it's time to start a new project. Your crew has the opportunity to build new homes or construct a civic project. Your friend Pura suggests you build homes. He reminds you that all homes in the city follow a similar pattern and are easy to build. Also, the new homes will be close to your neighborhood. That means you'll have a shorter walk to and from work.

"Let's see what the civic project involves," suggests Kalibasa, another friend. "It would be something that benefits the whole community rather than just individual families."

To work on homes, turn to page 84.
To work on civic buildings, turn to page 86.

You decide to be a farmer because you want to provide the people of Harappa with delicious and healthy foods. Some farmers grow crops. They raise grains such as wheat and barley, which can be used to make various dishes. They also grow legumes such as peas, chickpeas, and lentils, which can be cooked different ways and included in stews.

Some crop farmers focus on growing fruits. These include dates, grapes, figs, and mangos. Others grow sesame to make edible oil, and spices such as turmeric, ginger, and cinnamon.

But crop farming isn't your only option. Some farmers focus on raising animals for meat. The main animal raised is cattle, but some farmers raise goats, sheep, and chickens.

It's a tough decision. Do you want to raise animals or grow crops?

To raise animals, turn to page 88.
To grow crops, turn to page 89.

You tell Pura and Kalibasa that you'd prefer to work on a house this time. To your delight, they agree.

The first order of business is making bricks. You and Pura form bricks out of mud and grass. Then you use flat tools to size and smooth them. Meanwhile, Kalibasa stokes a big fire inside a large oven. As the bricks are ready, you slide them into the oven to bake. By baking the bricks, they become water-resistant. This is important in the Indus Valley since the river floods regularly.

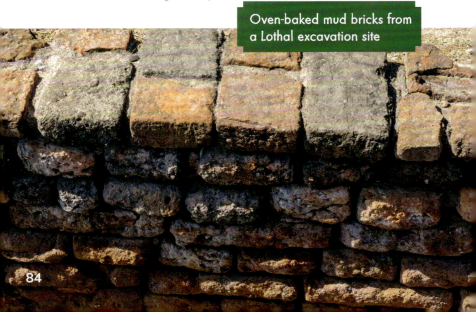

Oven-baked mud bricks from a Lothal excavation site

Within a few days, the pile of completed bricks grows tall. When the final bricks are placed in the oven, you switch your focus to the home's well. You take turns digging and hauling out the dirt.

As you finish your work on the well, you learn that your crew will be split to tackle two new tasks. One group will work on the sewage tunnels. These tunnels will connect this new house and neighborhood to the existing tunnels running under most of the city.

The other group will help build this home's upstairs. Now that the main floor is complete, that part of the house needs to be finished.

Which task do you want to tackle—the sewage lines or the upstairs?

>   To work on the sewage lines, turn to page 91.
>   To work upstairs, turn to page 93.

"I've built enough houses," you say. "Let's see what civic project they have for us."

You talk to your crew boss and learn that a wall is being built outside of the city. Not only will it protect the city from seasonal flooding, but it will also discourage invaders. Even though your city has never been attacked, it's important to protect it.

When you get to the construction site, you, Pura, and Kalibasa are tasked with working on a high part of the wall. Your job is to carry sacks of bricks up a ladder to the top. It's dangerous work. You try not to look down as you climb the ladder with one hand while balancing a heavy bag with the other.

Pura reaches the top ahead of you. While he carries his bag to a crew that is placing bricks, you look down the long ladder. Below you is Kalibasa. Below him are several more workers carrying bricks.

When you reach the top of the wall, you take a moment to catch your breath. Then you look down at Kalibasa. He smiles up at you as he climbs the last rungs of the ladder.

"We should have chosen to work on a house," he jokes, huffing.

As Kalibasa tries to heave his bag of bricks onto the wall, his smile turns into a look of surprise. He has lost his balance, and his hand slips off the ladder! Instantly, you know he will either fall to his death or drop his bricks on the men below him.

You only have a split second to react. You can either grab the bag of bricks or try to grab your friend's hand.

To grab the bricks, turn to page 94.
To try to grab your friend's hand, turn to page 95.

You decide to raise animals. Soon, your farm includes dairy cows as well as buffalo, sheep, goats, and chickens. You also have a grove of date palm trees, which produce delicious dates to eat and sell. But other than that, you don't grow other crops on your land. You trade meat in exchange for grain to feed the animals. You use an irrigation canal connected to the river to give your trees and animals water.

As the summer wears on, you notice that the irrigation ditch is getting lower. Before long, it is totally dry. The date trees wilt in the hot sun, and the animals stand around with their tongues lolling out. You need to get some water onto your farm—fast. You could dig your canal deeper, but the process could take weeks. Or you could perform a religious ritual in hopes of bringing more rain sooner.

To start digging, turn to page 97.
To try the ritual first, turn to page 99.

You decide to raise crops. You know you will enjoy working the land and seeing your livelihood literally sprout from the ground.

You grow several foods through the summer, including rice, beans, and peas. In the winter, you use the same land to grow wheat and barley. This smart technique helps keep the ground fertile. As different nutrients go into the soil, your farm remains productive all year long.

But by the tenth summer, a drought strikes. The cotton trees become brittle and produce little cotton. The rice, bean, and pea plants also look shorter than they should at this time of year. You fear they may not produce much at all. Furthermore, this is the third summer out of the last five that has been unusually dry. The world's climate seems to be changing.

One night after dinner, you talk things over with your family.

Turn the page.

"I've heard that farther downstream the droughts have not been so bad," you tell your wife.

"I've heard that too," she says. Then she mentions the new people from the north who have been immigrating into the city lately. "Can we trust these people? Perhaps we should move south," she says.

Moving would be a major undertaking. Selling the farm, packing up, and leaving friends would be hard on your family. It would also be costly. Maybe you should stick it out another year. But can you risk it?

To move, turn to page 100.
To stick it out another year, turn to page 101.

You decide to work on the sewage lines. First, you hitch an ox to a big plow blade. Then you lead it slowly along a path from the house to the common sewer under the street. The ox groans as you holler to urge it onward.

With the initial path cut, you and the other men use shovels to dig deeper and even out the sewer line. This process takes several days. By the time you finish, a large stack of baked bricks has been delivered to the site.

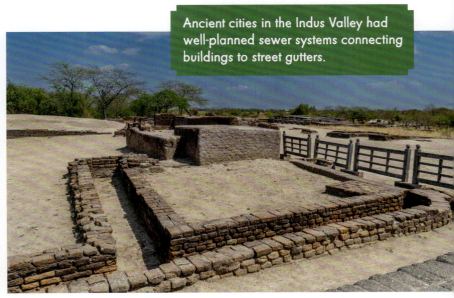

Ancient cities in the Indus Valley had well-planned sewer systems connecting buildings to street gutters.

Turn the page.

Using a sophisticated balance device, Pura weighs the bricks against large square stones that act as counterweights. In this manner, he can dole out the exact number of bricks needed for each sewer line. Then you, Kalibasa, and the rest of the crew line the sewer with bricks and tiles. These materials make the sewer watertight and allow wastewater to flow to the river.

When your work is complete, you smile with satisfaction. The family that lives here will be very comfortable.

THE END

To follow another path, turn to page 11.
To learn more about the Indus Civilization, turn to page 103.

You decide to tackle the project upstairs. You start by building brick walls to form rooms. Then you construct windows that are angled to catch cool breezes from the river and funnel them into the rooms. The windows act as natural air conditioners, which are very important in the hot river valley.

As you work, you think of the history of your city. A crew much like your own must have built the home you moved into. When you take a short break, you sit on this home's flat roof and look out over the incredible city. It is neat, clean, orderly, safe, and equitable. You feel good about the part you play in this community.

THE END

To follow another path, turn to page 11.
To learn more about the Indus Civilization,
turn to page 103.

Kalibasa is a close friend, but you can't risk more people getting hurt or killed. You quickly grab his bag of bricks. But as you lift, you lose your balance and tip forward.

Suddenly, it feels like you, Kalibasa, and the bricks will all tumble onto the men below. Then the weight of the bricks lessens. Pura has come up and grabbed them as well. The two of you heft them onto the wall, and—to your relief—Kalibasa regains his grip on the ladder.

Looking down below, you see the face of the next man climbing up. He looks shocked and relieved at the same time. It was a close call, but your teamwork prevented a tragedy. In that same way, you'll use teamwork to finish this wall and protect the lives of everyone in Harappa too.

THE END

To follow another path, turn to page 11.
To learn more about the Indus Civilization,
turn to page 103.

Kalibasa has been a close friend for a long time. In a flash, you snatch his flailing wrist. As you do, his bag slips from his grip and the bricks tumble out.

After you help Kalibasa up the last rungs of the ladder, both of you look down. Because the bricks scattered, many men were hit.

At first, it looks like most of the men took glancing blows. But then you see a worker on the ladder start to wobble.

You realize the worker's head is bleeding just as he slips from the ladder and plummets to the ground. You and Kalibasa both turn away, not wanting to see the man's final moments.

For the next few days, you try to continue with the job. But you can't rid your mind of your fallen coworker.

Turn the page.

Eventually, you ask to be transferred to a job working on a citadel. It will be the seat of government activity. It's on a high mound in the upper part of town.

You and Kalibasa never again talk about the incident on the wall. But both of you are haunted by it for the rest of your lives.

THE END

To follow another path, turn to page 11.
To learn more about the Indus Civilization, turn to page 103.

You hitch a couple zebus to your plow and start digging into the canal. After several passes, the canal is barely deeper. You realize you need help. So, you hitch up a cart and ride to your neighbor's farm downriver. Your neighbor walks out to meet you when he sees you coming.

"I saw you working on your canal this morning," he says.

"It's slow going," you reply. "How is yours?"

"Dry as a bone," he replies.

You suggest that you help each other, and he agrees. He brings his plow and two oxen up to your farm. Over several days, you work together to deepen the canal.

One morning, before your neighbor arrives, you see a trickle of water running through your canal. You run your plow through one more time, and the trickle increases.

Turn the page.

An irrigation canal supplying water to crops in present-day Pakistan

You breathe a sigh of relief. Your animals and trees are still in distress, but at least they will survive.

Later that day, you tell your neighbor you've got water and can begin work on his canal. You just hope this string of droughts comes to an end next year.

THE END

To follow another path, turn to page 11.
To learn more about the Indus Civilization, turn to page 103.

You do some chants and burn some incense in front of a small bronze figurine of a woman. She is a symbol of fertility that you keep near the well in your home. Like others in the community, you believe that honoring her in this way might increase the chances of rain.

After several days, however, no rain comes. Your irrigation canal remains dry. A dairy cow dies, and the trees produce no dates. You will have to deepen that canal for sure, now.

Meanwhile, some of your neighbors are moving south to areas with more reliable rainfall. You realize you may need to do that too. You just hope you don't lose everything to this drought before you do so.

THE END

To follow another path, turn to page 11.
To learn more about the Indus Civilization, turn to page 103.

You and your wife agree that the floods your fields need can no longer be relied upon in this area. You sell your land and many of your animals. Then you pack up and travel south.

After several weeks, you arrive in a town where you can buy some land. The journey was hard on your whole family, but the river floods your new farm fields when spring arrives. The smooth, glistening field of water is a beautiful sight. Not only does the flooding water your crops, but it also deposits nutrient-rich silt from the river.

It's going to be a good crop yield this year, but you're still nervous. Your new neighbors are already talking about how the floods have been less reliable here too. You may have to move again as the climate continues to change.

THE END

To follow another path, turn to page 11.
To learn more about the Indus Civilization, turn to page 103.

"We will stick it out another year," you say to your family. "We are good farmers. We can make this work."

Indeed, you manage a decent harvest in the fall. It's smaller than usual, but enough to get by.

Still, it stings a little when a government official comes to take some of your rice for taxes. But you know it's for a good cause, especially with droughts affecting crop yields. The city puts it in a granary to save in case of famine. It may need that emergency rice sooner than later to help everyone in your area.

And that includes the newest citizens from the north. It turns out they are a peaceful people. They also bring new skills and labor to your city.

THE END

To follow another path, turn to page 11.
To learn more about the Indus Civilization,
turn to page 103.

Chapter 5
THE END OF THE INDUS CIVILIZATION

The Indus Civilization was located along the Indus River system in modern-day India and Pakistan. It began around 5500 BCE as an agricultural society that raised animals and crops and made tools. Over time, the people of the Indus Valley established trade with Mesopotamia and other civilizations.

By 2600 BCE, the Indus people had built several major cities and hundreds of minor ones. There is no evidence of local or centralized governments. But every city was built in a uniform way, so scholars believe the people shared a set of common ideas that led to a unified culture.

Around 1900 BCE, the Indus Civilization began to decline. This decline happened around the same time people from the north migrated into the Indus Valley. In the 1800s, some researchers believed these people conquered the Indus people. Today, that theory has been completely ruled out. There is no evidence that any war or violence occurred in the area. Furthermore, the newcomers were probably Indo-Iranians who peacefully joined the Indus culture.

Meanwhile, researchers are still unsure why the Indus Civilization declined. It may have been spurred by the Ghaggar-Hakra River drying up. This intermittent river flows during the rainy monsoon season. Many people who depended on the Ghaggar-Hakra River would have had to find somewhere else to live. In other words, climate change may have forced people to move to better places.

An ancient stepwell in Dholavira, one of the largest known cities belonging to the Indus Civilization

A decline in trade may have also played a role in the end of the Indus Civilization. Both Egypt and Mesopotamia were engaged in conflicts during this time. These conflicts would have made it hard for the Indus people to trade with them and get the goods they needed to survive.

Whatever the cause, by 1600 or 1500 BCE the cities of the Indus had been abandoned. The people had moved farther south, into modern-day India. Future excavations of the region will certainly help scholars understand more about this incredible society.

TIMELINE OF THE INDUS CIVILIZATION

5500–2900 BCE—Pre-Harappan. Agricultural development and the creation of tools and pottery occurs in this early period.

2900-2600 BCE—Early Harappan. People live in small villages along the water. Ports, docks, and warehouses are built. Trade is established between Indus cities and to Mesopotamia, Iran, and Central Asia.

2600–1900 BCE—Mature Harappan. Cities are built, including the major cities Harappa and Mohenjo-daro. Cities are all built according to the same model, on a uniform grid pattern oriented to the cardinal points of north, south, east, and west. Cities have wells, sewage systems, bricks of uniform size, dockyards, granaries, protective walls, and public facilities. Harappans learn to work with metals, including bronze, copper, lead, and tin. They create crafts such as pottery and figurines of humans and animals. They use ox carts for trade over land and flat-bottomed boats for trade by sea.

1900–1500 BCE—Late Harappan. People from the Iranian Plateau and Central Asia begin immigrating. The civilization begins to decline, most likely due to climate change that causes flooding, drought, and famine, as well as a decline in trade.

1500–600 BCE—Post-Harappan. The people abandon the cities.

MORE ABOUT THE INDUS CIVILIZATION

>>> Historians do not know if the people of the Indus Valley were religious. Figurines and statuettes have been discovered, many of which are of women, often holding babies, which may have been suggesting fertility. The Great Bath in Mohenjo-daro may have been used for purification rituals or simply as a social place to bathe.

>>> The people of the Indus Valley are sometimes called Harappans after the site where the culture was first identified. It is believed that they were a peaceful people who did not engage in warfare, but some scholars consider this a myth. There is no evidence of conflict with other peoples, but this may be simply because the Indus Valley was relatively isolated. The weapons found at archaeological sites could have been used for hunting or for fighting.

>>> The Harappans domesticated cattle and other animals, including chickens, goats, sheep, and buffalo, to raise for food. They also hunted game birds, antelope, gazelles, deer, and boars, and they caught fish and shellfish. Meat was the main staple of their diet.

THE INDUS CIVILIZATION TODAY

Due to their obviously high level of technological and civic sophistication, the Indus Civilization is already considered one of the three greatest ancient civilizations, along with ancient Egypt and Mesopotamia. For that reason, scholars are very interested in learning more about this fascinating society.

A visitor exploring artifacts at a museum in Mohenjo-daro

To that end, excavation at the sites in the area of the Indus Civilization continues today. For example, a recent excavation in the Kachchh district in western India revealed an ancient settlement with pottery that is unique to the area.

While researchers have uncovered what appears to be a written language, they have not been able to translate it yet. So, we don't have any written history for the people. Everything we know about the civilization comes from the physical sites and materials that have been excavated. Documents found in Mesopotamia refer to ships coming from Dilmun, Magan, and Meluhha. It is believed that the term Meluhha refers to the Harappan Civilization.

A stamp seal from the Indus Civilization (left) and its modern-day impression

Some of the most common artifacts found in the Indus Valley are soapstone seals about one inch square, carved with characters and drawings. It is believed these were used as identifiers and could be used when signing contracts and in trade.

GLOSSARY

archaeologist (ar-kee-AH-luh-jist)—a scientist who studies how people lived in the past

artisan (AR-tuh-zuhn)—a skilled worker, especially one whose occupation requires hand skill

bronze (BRAHNZ)—a metal made of copper and tin; bronze has a gold-brown color

caravan (CARE-uh-van)—a group of people traveling together for safety

casting (KAST-ing)—making an object by pouring melted metal into a mold

citadel (SIT-uh-del)—a fortress, usually on high ground, protecting or forming a major part of a city

civic (SIV-ik)—relating to a city or town, especially its government

fertility (fur-TIL-uh-tee)—relating to the ability to have babies

granary (GRAY-nuh-ree)—a place to store grain

irrigation (ihr-uh-GAY-shuhn)—suppling water to crops using a system of pipes or channels

lapis lazuli (LA-puhs LA-zuh-lee)—a bright blue rock used for decoration and jewelry

mold (MOHLD)—a hollow container used to give shape to melted metal or another material when it cools and hardens

ritual (RICH-oo-uhl)—a ceremony involving a set of religious actions

soapstone (SOHP-stohn)—a soft rock consisting largely of talc

zebu (ZEE-boo)—a breed of domesticated oxen from India

READ MORE

Green, Sara. *Ancient India.* Minneapolis: Bellwether Media, 2020.

Lynch, Seth. *Ancient India.* Buffalo, NY: Enslow Publishing, 2025.

Reynolds, Donna. *Ancient India Revealed.* New York: Cavendish Square Publishing, 2023.

INTERNET SITES

The Ancient Indus Valley Civilization
harappa.com

National Geographic Kids: India
kids.nationalgeographic.com/geography/countries/article/india

World History Encyclopedia: Introduction to the Indus Valley Civilization
youtube.com/watch?v=lYQ9P0k7MoA

ABOUT THE AUTHOR

Eric Braun is a children's author and editor. He has written dozens of books on many topics, and one of his books was read by an astronaut on the International Space Station for kids on Earth to watch. Eric lives in Minneapolis, Minnesota, where you can usually find him on his bike.

BOOKS IN THIS SERIES

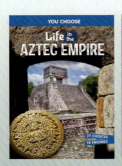
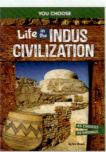
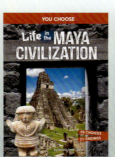